In God's Perfect Hands

```
IØ159317
```

Copyright© 2014 Amanda Matthews

Dedication

This book is dedicated to all the people who know that God is able to do all things. For those who are not sure, God is very much real, and on the throne in heaven.

Acknowledgements

I would like to give praise and love to the Most High God for blessing me with my talents, life, love, and His favor. None of this would be possible without you. I love you Abba Father.

To my mother Leatrice Matthews, for always being there when the storms of life were raging. You will always be one of my greatest inspirations.

To my sweet children, Ray, Hannah, Daniel, and Keara, you guys are always in my thoughts, heart, mind, and prayer. Mommy loves you always.

Inside the Life

You do not know about the hunger
The feeling of never being full
Someone in this life
Always feeding you bull
You work your fingers to the bone
Working for that extra pull
Standing on the corners
Helping the brothers
Helping the sisters
Come home to God
The man that came to us
Gave us life
Who is there for us
Through our time of strife
I am tired of the devil
Pulling the wool over our eyes
When will we realize
One day we will be free
From the trap of money
From the surroundings of poverty
The pains in our hearts
Will soon diminish
Inside the life
All things will change

In God's Perfect Hands

Prowler

A finger to touch
The center of your lips
To speak no more
For they can hear you
Every move that you make
They know
Counting all of your footprints
Two by two
Slowly
He is watching you
Cursing
Laughing
Casting his spell
Wishing you death
But God is able to do all things

No Matter

You are the love of life
My heart belongs to you
I am proud to be your wife
You are my dream come true
No matter near or far
No matter night or day
I love you for who you are
In all types of ways
You are in my heart's desire
No matter night or day
No matter the hour
I will love you anyway

In God's Perfect Hands

God is My Everything

My only true love
IS the Lord Jesus Christ
The center of my life
God is my best friend
HE believes in me
He does not judge me
For the color of my skin
The sound of my voice
Only the person that is within
Your heart
Your soul
Your spirit
Lord you are my everything
I must tell the world
About the joy that bring in my life
Lord I love you so
I want the whole world to know

In God's Perfect Hands

Reality
In the life of the homeless man
The world refuses to understand
We need to do
All that we can
To save the people of the land
Hemans are slowly dying
Innocent children are really crying
We should never give up trying
To change the situations
Of all the nations
WE should join in unity
People suffer in misery
They do not have food to eat
The do not have shoes on their feet
They do not have clothes to keep them warm
Where is their protection from disease?
I am asking heaven please
There are humans that do not have a place to stay
They are danger every single day
They lay in the streets
Sleep in the trash
Beg for dear life
Lord please end this strife
We must remember them soon

In God's Perfect Hands

Children are born without the love
Coming from heaven above
Sweet and soft as a dove
They are abused
They are accused
How can we lose the future of
tomorrow?
Protect from pain
Keep them from sorrow
I should keep trying
Our children are constantly dying
A young girl sniffs poison to get high
She will surely be the one to die
I contemplate asking myself why
There is no simple reply
Small children are being lost
We must help them at all cost
Elderly people unable to see
Are being mistreated constantly
They are alone
Locked up in a home
Once grown
Now they are old
A precious story that is always told
God is in control

If I Could Fly
If I could fly
I would fly
Like an angel
High in the air
Soaring so far
Away from here
Away from there
Tomorrow may never come
For you
For me
Without your love
What would I do?
If I could
I would leave
This sinful world
Not by death but by grace
I would fly
With my angel's wings of gold
If I could

In God's Perfect Hands

Promise Land
I prayed for my family
One day that we will be
Tighter than a hand and glove
Someday we will walk
Down the old road of life
Mother
Father
Sister
Brother
Husband
Wife
Someday we will get
To the promise land

Remember Me

There has to be a better way
For us to make it through
Tomorrow does not represent today
All of hopes and dreams
Shatter before my eyes
Down to my knees
I soon realize
How much I need you in my life
To see you all the time
To see me through my pain
After all that has happened
The hurt still remains
How sad is my heart
How often do I cry?
My soul began to weaken
I feel as though
I want to die
I will make it at all cost
Please remember me
When I am gone

Misty Eyes

She sat crying with her tears
So much pain did she had over the years
No one loved her enough to know
Times were tough
She had to go
Through a lifetime
Malice, strife, and ongoing trauma
She had an innocence of most
melodrama
Cold was the world
Tired was her soul
Aching was her heart
For it was torn apart
Through rain and snow
Sun and shine
Surely she knew
All about the tears and cries
All about her sleepy misty eyes

Jesus

In God's Perfect Hands

Believe in what God has said
May your sleep be peaceful?
When you go to bed
May your dreams be sweet with grace?
May a smile be on your face?
The entire world
Is his glory
I will tell you about his story
Born to the virgin named Mary
Son of the Most High
Lord of the worlds
Son of perfection
A light of the earth
Sinless
Prefect
From the birth
A friend
A brother
A father and a mother
Helper
Doctor
Lawyer
Keeper

Life

In God's Perfect Hands

My poor brother
My poor sister
Oppressed by poverty
Life got you down
Making you frown
Trouble in the third degree
Reach out
Reach out
All things will come through him
When your way is dark
Believe
For the Most High
Life!
Life!
Life!
My dear sweet Lord
Why?
Are the oppressed more oppressed?
Why are the poor more oppressed?
Living in poverty
Trouble in the third degree
The man with richness
Looks down on the impoverished man
I still do not understand
Why my brother
Why my sister
Has to have pain
The Lord is our Savior
Helping us through the rain
Shine on

In God's Perfect Hands

Be merry
Shout the highest praise
The Lord will be there
To heal all of your troubled ways

Thanking Him

In God's Perfect Hands

Like the sun that shines in the day
The moon shimmers in the night
Lord I thank you graciously
Through my heart soul and mind
A God that is true and divine
One that understands
That knows what is true
That knows the strength of your youth
My Father you are the light

My Love

In God's Perfect Hands

You are the one
That my heart beats for
You are the man
That I adore
I sing because of you
Your smile is like the golden sun
Your eyes shimmer like the moon
They twinkle like the stars in heaven
My love for you is pure
I have never been so sure
About the way that I feel
Our love is real

The Return

In God's Perfect Hands

Somewhere in a distant place
I know that I saw his face
Holes in His hands and feet
A thorn crown on his head
I felt a breath of warm air
A voice whispered
As if someone was there
A cross was in the mist
Could Jesus be returning soon?

I Imagine

In God's Perfect Hands

No one ever understood
The voice of the kid
They remember the bad things
That the kid did
The voice of a child is always unheard
You are silent
When it comes to your word
Did they ever take the time?
To read between the lines
They felt as though
They were strong at reading minds
No one else listens to a voice of a kid
All they remember is the bad things that
you did
When you wake up to see
You are really on your own
Your best intentions are the ones that
you own
Better to be alone
Than a fool for someone else
Better to be real with yourself
Than to live in misery with someone else
Knowing that they may never
understand a kid's word
Better to be silent
Than to try desperately to be heard
I imagine being free

To be me

In God's Perfect Hands

For the world to see
To understand that life
Is not always fair
The truth is
You are the only one there
I imagine being whole
My own person
In happiness and in pain
Nothing to lose
Only life to gain
Smiles that creep
When you go to sleep
I imagine
A world without sin
HE was born before my strife begin
A stumbling block
A rock
Of salvation
A father
To all the nations

How Did I Survive?

In God's Perfect Hands

I have given my heart to you
Trusting
That you would always be true
Hoping
That life would be fair
Late at night
Thoughts of you
Come to my mind
I lay alone
Tortured
By memories
How did I survive?
This wretched love affair
I no longer dream
Sweet thoughts
Only the night mare of our love remains
My soul is troubled
My heart is torn to pieces
I wish daylight
Would flee from me
How did I survive loving you?
How did I survive?

Thank you Lord

In God's Perfect Hands

Thank you Lord for blessing me
Helping me through the storm
Keeping me safe
Keeping me from harm
Glorious heavenly Father
This holy light of mine
Thank you Lord for understanding me
When your heart is overwhelmed
You have brought me joy
When I was down
You opened up the door
I thank you for blessing me

To God

My God
You are my life
Without you
I am eternally dead
I live and breathe to serve you
My heart
Belongs to you
My spirit
Yearns for your presence
My temple
Needs you
All my life
Is devoted to you
My mind
Is filled with thoughts of you
I adore and love you
I need you for all eternity

The Sunlight in Your Eyes

In God's Perfect Hands

I long to feel
The sunlight in your hair
I imagine seeing you there
In my arms all tiny and sweet
A perfect little angel
Someone God has sent to comfort me
Make my world happy
I will have pain for you
Loving you
Unconditionally
You are the reason that I live
For you I will do all things
I will wait on you
Until the end of time

Perfect Dream

In God's Perfect Hands

There is no greater love
Than the one that you give
For you I breathe
For you I live
I open my heart to the one that makes
me whole
My perfect dream comes true
If you were never told
My love runs deep for you
Like a flowing river
Flowing fast and free
Our love will always be
A great romance that will come alive
I am giving you half the chance
I will provide
The life of true wonder
A strong desire for you
You are my perfect dream come true

Perfect Dream

In God's Perfect Hands

There is no greater love
Than the one that you give
For you I breathe
For you I live
I open my heart to the one that makes
me whole
My perfect dream comes true
If you were never told
My love runs deep for you
Like a flowing river
Flowing fast and free
Our love will always be
A great romance that will come alive
I am giving you half the chance
I will provide
The life of true wonder
A strong desire for you
You are my perfect dream come true

Believe

In God's Perfect Hands

My dear Lord
I wait for the day
When the trumpet will sound
When the saints will claim victory
I believe in that day
I believe that my dreams will come true
I believe in you

Bronze Flower Shop

In God's Perfect Hands

A place where African violets
Dance across the floor
Lilies swim
In the glass ponds
Roses spread around the room
Sunflowers shine a wonderful aroma
Of grand elegance
Daises fill the windows
With such delight
Chrysanthemums are the gateways to
heaven

A Praying Woman

In God's Perfect Hands

Lord
O merciful and beneficent ruler
Thank you majestic Father
How I love to call your name
Lord
We come to this land
My mother struggled to raise me
From the dust of poverty
My Father Lord
Never got to know me
Even today
He has nothing to say
From the wounds of my heart
To the scars of my soul
No one knows the truth
Have mercy
Just like an angel that has lost her way
The pain can be felt throughout the
community
Please make a way

A Sister's Call

In God's Perfect Hands

A lil' 'black girl
Once said to me
Will this world
Ever be free
From the sin that we face
Deep within
The African American race
She claimed to be
A mother at an early age
The child appeared to be
Trapped in a lonely cage
Her eyes were clear
As the flowing water of a river
Makes me shiver
Youth
Gone for life
Until the next life
I shall remember the day
I heard my sister's call

For You

In God's Perfect Hands

For you
I would climb the highest mountain
Swim in the deepest sea
Sail
High in the sky
For the world to see
I would sign your name
On the pages of my heart
Position untold
Position unfold
Promise me my love
We will never part
For you I would die
I would never let you go
You will always be in my heart

Feels like Rain

In God's Perfect Hands

The rains from heaven
Fall like fire
As lightning streaks
Across the sky
Darkness flows into the sea
As the tears silently roll by
Rivers the color of scarlet
As the blood of men flow
The sand of time
The light of night
Broken hands do know
The morning is sunny
The night is a gloom
Morning comes
Oh so soon

Homeless

In God's Perfect Hands

A man on the corner
Selling bread for a dime
Life is passing surely
He is running out of time
How sad is his heart
A cardboard box his home
Many worlds apart
Standing alone
Often the tears flow
More than he can stand
In reality life goes on
For this homeless man
The child next door
Only thirteen years of age
Suffers from hunger
Her mind a deadly cage
No food to eat
The water well runs dry
She feels sadness and defeat
Her life is all a lie
How can one so young
Hurt so bad
This is the life of the homeless

The Heartbeat of a Drum

In God's Perfect Hands

I hear the sound of a trumpet
The heartbeat of a drum
The claps of a people
A voice that will hum
Singing the praises of freedom
Shouting the joys of equality
Standing in harmony
Praying for the knowledge
I heard the sounds of misery
The beat of a drum
Cries of a people
A sad voice that hums
Moaning the pains of bondage
Yelling the sorrows of depression
Sitting in hell
Praying for the knowledge
I hear the sounds of the trumpet
The beat of a drum
Sounds of wings
Voices that hum
Singing the praises of freedom
Master No more tears for me!
Eternally free

If We Never Love Again

In God's Perfect Hands

You are the wind beneath my wings
You are the joy that my heart loves to
sing
I love the sweet sounds of your name
Without you I will never be the same
You are the sea
I am the rain
I would die
If we never loved again
You are the sun
That shines bright in the sky
See the happy tears that fall from my
eyes
You are the love that fills my soul
You are the silver
You are the gold
You are the sea
I am the rain
I would die
If we never love again

Did You Ever Think?

In God's Perfect Hands

Did you ever look at the word?
To read what it says
Look at the time?
At the lengths of our days
The way we stand on the brink of
destruction
Do you care about disease?
You should get down on your knees?
Thank God for your treasures
Lovers of the Lord
Not lovers of pleasure
Release the madness that lurk deep
within
What about the end?
Famines
Earthquakes
Rumors of wars
Do you think my brothers?
Have you thought my sisters?
Do you have a thought at all?
Did you ever think that we are the
people?
That God allowed to enjoy his creations?

The Return

In God's Perfect Hands

My Lord
Has long has it been?
Since you paid a visit
To a friend
From the Passover
To the resurrection
My honorable Prince
I have no objection
My dear Jesus
How have you been?
Preaching for years
About evil sin
That fills the earth
The world around you
Will soon be anew
My heavenly brother
How long will it be?
Before we are eternally free
Most of us are afraid to die
We gladly rejoice and testify
My Lord
When will you return?
When will humans ever learn?
The truth
About your untimely death
How much time have we left?
Tell me my prince
When we will know
About your trauma and woe

In God's Perfect Hands

Your eternal happiness
Described in the Bible best
I wait for your return
As a believer
I will gladly learn
About the truths that you told long ago
That is how I will know
I keep the faith while I wait
Knowing that it is wrong to hate
You love unconditionally
Caring for the people gently
I hope to be just like you
Godlike
Loving
Kind and true
Free from sin eternally!
Bondage will be gone totally!
My Lord
I look up to you
A man with a heart so true
A soul so pure
A spirit so strong
In your rest
IS where I belong
My Lord
My friend
My everything
Oh what joy your bring!
To many generations
In this world

To every man, women, boy, and girl.
We await your return.

*""Look, he is coming with the clouds,"
and "every eye will see him, even those
who pierced him"; and all peoples on
earth "will mourn because of him." So
shall it be! Amen."   (Revelation 1:7) NIV*